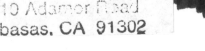

A New True Book

BASKETBALL

By Bert Rosenthal

Children's Press®
A Division of Grolier Publishing
New York   London   Hong Kong   Sydney
Danbury, Connecticut

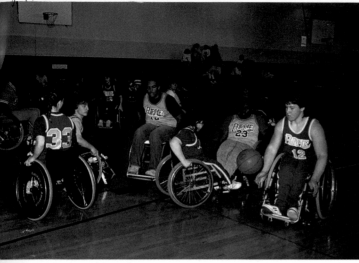

Handicapped players play
basketball from wheelchairs

PHOTO CREDITS

AllSport — 16 (top), 42; © Jonathan Daniel, cover, 12 (2 photos), 18, 28, 31 (right), 35 (bottom), 41 (right), 44; © Doug Pensinger, 7; © Gary Mook, 10; © Stephen Dunn, 14, 15, 24; © Brian Drake, 16 (bottom), 23, 35 (top); © Phil Sears, 20 (top left); © Rick Stewart / Focus West, 20 (bottom left); © J. D. Cuban, 20 (right), 31 (left), 33; © Tim Defrisco, 34 (top), © Jim Gund, 34 (bottom)

AP/Wide World Photos — 8 (2 photos), 37, 41 (left)

Naismith Memorial Basketball Hall of Fame — 4

Unicorn Stock Photos — © Ken Stevens, 2; © Issac Greenberg, 9

UPI/Bettmann Newsphotos — 22, 27, 38

Cover — 1993 NBA Final

Library of Congress Cataloging-in-Publication Data

Rosenthal, Bert.
    Basketball / by Bert Rosenthal.
        p. cm. — (A New true book)
    Includes index
    Summary: Explains the fundamental aspects of basketball including equipment, scoring, game rules, players and officials, and contrasts professional basketball with high school and college sport.
    ISBN 0-516-01080-8
    1. Basketball — Juvenile literature.
[1. Basketball]— I. Title.
GV885. 1.R67 1995   95-17425
796.323'2—dc20   CIP AC

CONTENTS

Doctor James Naismith, showing a young basketball
player some tips in the late 1800s

THE HISTORY OF BASKETBALL

The game of basketball
began in the United States
in 1891. It was invented by
Dr. James Naismith, a
physical education
instructor from Canada who
was teaching at the
International Young Men's
Christian Association
(YMCA) Training School in
Springfield, Massachusetts.

Basketball became popular because it was easy to learn and could be played by many students indoors during the cold winter months.

Today basketball is played all year-round. Although the game has changed a lot since 1891, thirteen of the original rules of play are included in today's rule books.

THE PLAYING AREA

A regulation basketball court is 94 feet long. In high school, the court may be only 84 feet long.

At each end of the court, there is a basket.

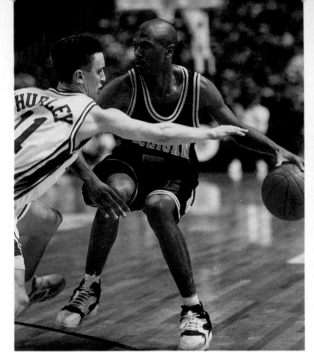
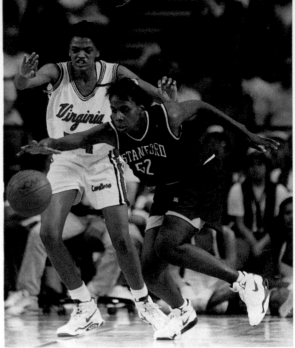

Players reach in to steal the ball. Left: Duke's Blue Devils and the Michigan Wolverines Right: Women's basketball between Stanford and Virginia

The court is divided into two halves. Once a team gets the ball, it must bring it across the half-court line within ten seconds. If it doesn't, the other team gets the ball.

8

A basketball is round and usually orange. It is 21 inches and weighs between 20 and 22 ounces. Girls, women, and some boys' high-school teams often use a smaller ball.

Players usually hold a basketball with two hands. That makes it easy to pass and shoot.

To score, a player must shoot the ball through the basket.
A score is called a "basket" or a "field goal."

THE PLAYERS

In basketball, there are
five players on each team.
There are two forwards, two
guards, and one center.
The center usually is the
tallest player on the team.
He tries to make rebounds.
That means he tries to get
the ball away from the other
team when the ball does
not go into the basket.

Left: Guard Dana Barros of the Philadelphia
76ers. Right: Bulls forwards Toni Kukoc (7)
and Scottie Pippin (33)

The guards usually are
the shortest team members.
They bring the ball down the
court to their team's basket.
The forwards are taller
than the guards. They play
closer to the basket.

SCORING

A player shoots the ball through the basket. That usually counts for two points.

Sometimes a player makes a basket from 22 feet away. Then it counts for three points. The three-point basket — or field goal — is now used in

Nick Van Exel of the Los Angeles Lakers tries for a three-point basket.

professional, college, and most high-school games.

In pro games, each team is given 24 seconds to take a shot. The team might not take a shot

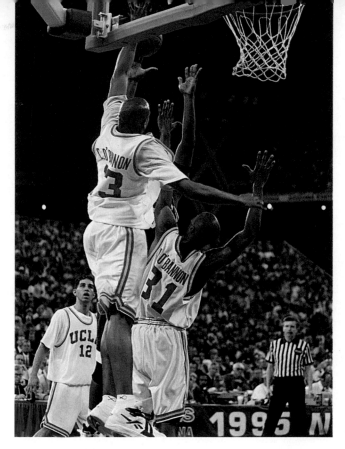

UCLA Bruins try
to block a shot.

within that time. Then the
other team is given the
ball.

In most college games,
the teams have 45
seconds to take a shot.

Above: Players from opposing teams go up for a rebound.
Below: Shaquille O'Neal of the Orlando Magic slams the
ball through the basket from above the rim.

RULES

After one team scores, the ball goes to the other team. That team puts the ball into play. Players start from under the basket where the score was made. They put the ball into play from the sidelines.

The player with the ball — usually a guard — moves toward the basket. He or she can dribble, or bounce, the

A player usually dribbles with his or her head up and eyes straight ahead so that he or she can see where to pass the ball.

ball. The player walks or runs while dribbling the ball. He or she can pass the ball to a teammate, or can shoot the ball at the basket. But the player cannot run while holding the ball with both hands.

OFFICIALS

There are several officials — or referees — in charge of each game. They run the game according to the rules.

Referees have many important jobs. They toss the ball up between two opposing players to start a game. This is called a

Referee (top left) shows where a foul has been committed. After a ref calls a held ball, he tosses the ball up between two opposing players (top right), who try to tap the ball to a teammate. A technical foul (left) can be called for fighting, unsportsmanlike conduct, or delay of game. It can be called on a coach, a player on the floor, or even a player sitting on the bench.

jump ball. They also call fouls.

To call a foul, a referee blows a whistle. This stops the play. Then he identifies the foul with hand or arm signals.

Referees also decide if a ball goes out of bounds — off the court — and which team touched the ball last.

FOULS

A foul occurs when a player holds, pushes, elbows, or charges into another team's player.

Armon Gilliam of the Philadelphia 76ers throws an elbow to the head of New Jersey Nets Jack Haley.

Charles Barkley
of the Phoenix
Suns at the free-
throw line

The player who was
fouled shoots from the foul
line, or free throw line.
This line is 15 feet from
the basket. If the player
makes this shot, it is worth
one point.

Patrick Ewing of the New York Knicks shooting a free throw

Sometimes a player is fouled while shooting a basket. Then the player can try two free throws.

In pro basketball, a player is taken out of the game after committing six fouls. In college and high school games, a player committing five fouls is taken out.

PLAYING TIME

Pro basketball games are divided into four quarters. Each quarter lasts 12 minutes. That makes a total of 48 minutes.

College games are divided into two halves. Each half is 20 minutes. That makes a total of 40 minutes.

High-school games last 32 minutes. They are divided

The scoreboard shows a tied game between the Atlanta Hawks and the Indiana Pacers. Can you tell in what period the game is, and how much time remains?

into four quarters of eight minutes each.

What if the game is tied at the end? Then it goes

Phil Jackson, coach of the Chicago Bulls, discusses last-minute strategy during a time-out.

into overtime. Professional and college teams play five-minute overtime periods. High-school teams play three-minute overtime periods.

The game ends if, at the end of any extra period, the score is not tied.

All teams are given short rest periods between halves of each game. They also rest before any overtime periods and during time outs.

DEFENSE

In pro basketball, each player must guard a player from the other team. That is called playing defense.

In college and high-school games, teams may use either a man-to-man defense or a zone defense.

In zone defense, a player guards a part of the court

On defense, players guard closely. Right: Michael Jordan tries to force a bad pass or dribble, which can lead to a steal.

rather than one player.
Any player in that area
must be guarded.

PROFESSIONAL BASKETBALL

There is one major pro league in the United States. It is called the National Basketball Association (NBA). It has two conferences, four divisions, and 29 teams.

Fifteen teams play in the Eastern Conference. Fourteen teams play in the Western Conference.

Los Angeles Lakers are in the Pacific Division of the Western Conference.

The Atlantic and Central Divisions are part of the Eastern Conference. The Midwest and Pacific Divisions are part of the Western Conference.

Eastern Conference

Atlantic Division
Boston Celtics
Miami Heat
New Jersey Nets
New York Knicks
Orlando Magic
Philadelphia 76ers
Washington Bullets

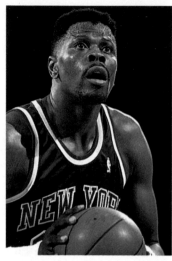

Patrick Ewing, New York Knicks

Central Division
Atlanta Hawks
Charlotte Hornets
Chicago Bulls
Cleveland Cavaliers
Detroit Pistons
Indiana Pacers
Milwaukee Bucks
Toronto Raptors

Larry Johnson, Charlotte Hornets

Western Conference

Midwest Division

Dallas Mavericks
Denver Nuggets
Houston Rockets
Minnesota
  Timberwolves
San Antonio Spurs
Utah Jazz
Vancouver Grizzlies

Mahmoud Abdul-Rauf, Denver Nuggets

Pacific Division

Golden State
  Warriors
Los Angeles Clippers
Los Angeles Lakers
Phoenix Suns
Portland Trail Blazers
Sacramento Kings
Seattle SuperSonics

Charles Barkley, Phoenix Suns

Pro teams play 82 games
during the regular season.
The 16 best teams continue
playing after the regular
season. Those teams
include the four division
champions. Six more teams
are picked from each
conference. They are the
teams with the next-best
records.

Those 16 teams go to the
playoffs. The first round of
the playoffs is a five-game
series. The first team to win
three games wins the series.

Chicago Bulls
Michael Jordan
dunks a shot
during the 1992
NBA Finals against
the Portland Trail
Blazers.

In the second round,
there are eight teams left.
Each series is seven
games. The first team
winning four games wins
the series.

Washington Bullets Pervis Ellison (43) and Orlando Magic
Greg Kite (34) go for a rebound.

In the third round, there are four teams left. Each series also is seven games. And again, the first team winning four games wins the series.

Then, two teams are left. They play the last seven-game series. This is called the NBA Finals. The first team winning four games is the NBA champion.

COLLEGE
BASKETBALL

Nearly every major college in the United States has a basketball team. Many have two teams, one for men and one for women.

Each year these teams compete in tournaments. About 750 schools in the National Collegiate Athletic Association (NCAA) sponsor men's basketball.

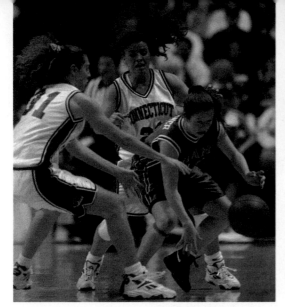

Left: A Big East Conference game between Connecticut and Miami. Right: Indiana playing in the 1992 NCCA tournament

About 550 schools sponsor women's teams.

College teams play between 25 and 30 games a season. After the regular season, there are championship tournaments. In the NCAA, 64 teams

compete in the Division I
tournament. Many of the
teams are conference
champions. There are also
tournaments for Division II
and Division III schools.

After the 64 teams
compete, 16 regional

champions remain. The regional champs compete until there are four finalists. The "Final Four" then meet in a doubleheader. The two remaining finalists then battle for the title of NCAA champions.

Playing and watching basketball is exciting. Whether the game is played on a professional, college, high-school, grade-school, or neighborhood level, it is a sport that can be fun for everyone.

Famous Professional Players

Kareem Abdul-Jabbar, Milwaukee Bucks, Los Angeles Lakers

Charles Barkley, Philadelphia 76ers, Phoenix Suns

Larry Bird, Boston Celtics

Wilt Chamberlain, Philadelphia/San Francisco Warriors, Philadelphia 76ers, Los Angeles Lakers

Julius Erving, Philadelphia 76ers

Magic Johnson, Los Angeles Lakers

Michael Jordan, Chicago Bulls

George Mikan, Minneapolis Lakers

Hakeem Olajuwan, Houston Rockets

Shaquille O'Neal, Orlando Magic

Bill Russell, Boston Celtics

Michael Jordan and Shaquille O'Neal

GLOSSARY

backboard (băk´ bord) — the flat sheet of wood or hard plastic to which a basket is attached

center (sĕn´ter) — the person who plays the middle position

commit (kă mĭt´) — to do something

contact (kŏn´takt) — to touch or come together

court (kort) — a marked off area where certain games are played

defense (dē´fence) — in basketball, to try to keep the other team from scoring

dribble (drĭb´il) — to move the basketball by bouncing it along the court

forward (for´word) — one of two players who, with the center, is usually in the front line of play

foul (fowl) — to do something in a basketball game that is against the rules

guard (gard) — one of two players who brings the ball to the front court

league (lēg) — a group of sport teams that play against one another

opponent (uh pō´nent) — in a game, the person who is on the other team

overtime (ō´ver tīm) — time that is beyond a set limit

professional (prō fesh´uh nul) — a person who is paid for playing a game

quarter (kwor´ter) — one of four time periods that make up a game.

rebound (rē´bound) — to get the ball after it bounces off the rim of the net

referee (rĕf er rē´) — the person in charge of the game who sees that the rules are followed

regulation (rĕg ū lā´shun) — a rule or law

score (skor) — to make a point in a game

series (sĭr´ēz) — a group of games that are played

time out — to take a break from playing a game

tournament (tur´nă ment) — a contest in which many competitors take part

zone (zōn) — in basketball, to guard a certain area of the court

INDEX

ABOUT THE AUTHOR

Bert Rosenthal has worked for the Associated Press (AP) for nearly 25 years. He has covered or written about virtually every sport. He was AP's pro basketball editor from 1973 until 1976. From 1974 until early 1980, he was the secretary-treasurer of the Professional Basketball Writers' Association of America.

Mr. Rosenthal is the author of The True Book of *Soccer* and books on Larry Bird and Sugar Ray Leonard. He has been a co-author on two books — *Pro Basketball Superstars of 1974* and *Pro Basketball Superstars of 1975*.

Mr. Rosenthal has been editor of HOOP Magazine, an official publication of the National Basketball Association, and an AP track and field editor. He is a frequent contributor to many basketball, football, and baseball magazines.